# Blairsville Junior High School
## Blairsville, Pennsylvania

# The First Book of THE INCAS

*Intihuantana, "the Hitching Place of the Sun," at Machu Picchu, is cut out of the living rock. It is thought that the priests of the sun judged the seasons by reading the shadows cast by this huge sundial.*

# The FIRST BOOK of
# THE INCAS

❖

## BY BARBARA L. BECK

### PICTURES BY PAGE CARY

**FRANKLIN WATTS, INC.**
575 Lexington Avenue • New York 10022

3039

JACKET PICTURE:
*Inca ruins at Machu Picchu*

Library of Congress Catalog Card Number: 66-10579
© Copyright 1966 by Franklin Watts, Inc.
Printed in the United States of America
by Polygraphic Company of America
2  3  4  5

# CONTENTS

# The First Book of THE INCAS

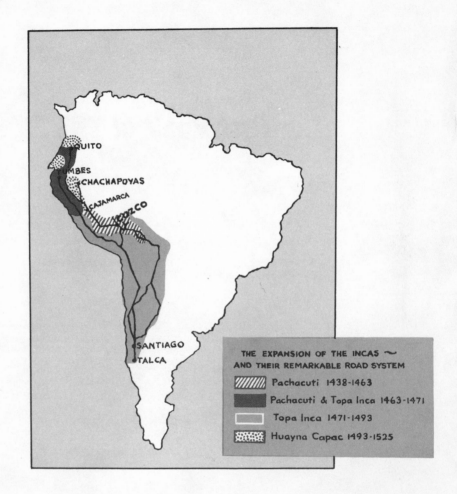

THE EXPANSION OF THE INCAS ～
AND THEIR REMARKABLE ROAD SYSTEM

Pachacuti 1438-1463

Pachacuti & Topa Inca 1463-1471

Topa Inca 1471-1493

Huayna Capac 1493-1525

QUITO
UMBES
CHACHAPOYAS
CAJAMARCA
CUZCO
SANTIAGO
TALCA

*The Inca Empire*

# DISCOVERING A CIVILIZATION

About seven hundred years ago, around A.D. 1200, the first Inca people entered Cuzco, in what is now Peru. In time, this city, high in the Andes Mountains of South America, became the center of a great empire. We know very little about what happened there between the years 1200 and 1438, for this period is one recalled mostly by legends and vague history about the first eight rulers of the Inca people. The ninth ruler, Pachacuti, is considered the first real empire ruler. From 1438, then, to 1532 — a period of less than one hundred years — the Incas forged an empire that extended two thousand miles up and down South America and included some six million people. But in 1532 this mighty empire was dramatically conquered by a tiny force of Spanish soldiers and became a Spanish possession.

The land of the Incas extended from the present-day cities of Quito in Colombia to below Santiago in Chile, and included parts of what are now Ecuador, Peru, Bolivia, Chile, and Argentina.

Peru, homeland of the Incas, has three kinds of country: coastal deserts, high mountains, and steaming jungles. The coastal desert of Peru is pierced by more than thirty prominent river valleys. Here lived many of the tribes who had important civilizations before Inca history began.

In contrast to the coastal deserts are the Andes Mountains, home of the Incas and other, earlier peoples.

1

Tumbling eastward down this backbone of mountains are two gigantic rivers which empty into the Amazon. Here, in the surrounding jungles, were fierce tribes of headhunters and savages. The coastal desert and the mountains, to the edge of the jungle, became the realm of the Incas.

The word "Inca" means several things. In Quechua (KESH-wa), a native Peruvian language, it means "lord." Some scholars say it means "conqueror" or "king," or was a title similar to "pharaoh." In their day the people of the Inca were not called Incas. This is a name that has been given them by historians.

Finding out about the Inca people and those who lived before them has been difficult, for none of these peoples had a system of writing. But because the Incas were conquered by the Spanish, who could write, there are some early records. These were written by (1) soldier-secretaries of the conquistadores, the Spanish conquerors; (2) lesser Spanish officials and soldiers; (3) the Spanish-educated, half-Inca, half-Spanish writers; (4) priests of the Catholic church, who came to Peru to teach Christianity.

Perhaps one of the best-known early writers was Pedro de Cieza de León, a Spanish soldier. Although Cieza de León was not a scholar, his books contain accurate information about the Incas. In traveling some three thousand miles through Inca country during the days of the Conquest, Cieza de León set down every detail of his journey.

Garcilaso de la Vega was born of a royal Inca mother and a noble Spanish father. Even though he was educated in Spain, Garcilaso

*Self-portrait of Felipe Guamán Poma de Ayala, Inca-Spanish chronicler who wrote the book,* The First New Chronicle and Good Government. *He is shown talking with an Indian. Poma de Ayala's book was lost, but was finally found in 1908 in the Royal Library at Copenhagen, Denmark. (Redrawn from Poma de Ayala.)*

de la Vega had a deep knowledge of his mother's people and had learned much about early Inca history. His book *The Royal Commentaries of the Incas* contains valuable but not always accurate information about legends, customs, and conquests.

Another Spanish-Inca author, Felipe Guamán Poma de Ayala, wrote a book between the years 1560 and 1599. In it he drew many pictures of the Incas, showing their costumes and their ways. Some of the pictures in this book you are reading have been redrawn from Poma de Ayala's drawings.

In addition to early writings by the Spanish and by Spanish-educated Incas there are more recent histories. In 1847, William H. Prescott published his book *The History of the Conquest of Peru.*

3

*Archeologists number the fallen stones of a building after they have discovered where they originally belonged. Then the native workers have the job of putting the building back together again by following the order of these numbers. This reconstruction is at Machu Picchu.*

This famous work was followed by Sir Clements Robert Markham's *A History of Peru* and his translations of several Spanish chronicles.

History is one source of our knowledge; archeology is another. In 1863, E. George Squier went to Peru to represent the United States government. Squier explored and dug into ruins in many parts of Peru, and later wrote a book about his findings. He was followed by the German archeologist Max Uhle. For forty years Uhle poked into tombs and burial holes. He collected thousands of pieces of pottery, and tools, weapons, jewelry, and weaving. His collection is world famous today.

In 1911, Hiram Bingham, another scholar of Peruvian history, came upon Machu Picchu. The discovery of this Inca stronghold high in the Andes Mountains sparked new interest in Peru. Bingham's companion, Philip Ainsworth Means, remained in Peru and later wrote two important books: *Ancient Civilizations of the Andes* and *Fall of the Inca Empire and the Spanish Rule in Peru, 1530-1780.*

In recent years many Inca ruins have been unearthed by archeologists. By studying how the Incas buried their dead, painted their pottery, wove their clothing, and made their roads and buildings, the archeologists have learned a great deal about the Incas' mighty civilization.

There is much more to be discovered in Peru. Hidden on the sides of the great gorges in the glistening, snowcapped Andes, or on some high plateau, more Inca ruins are waiting to tell their secrets.

# EARLY PERU

Thousands of years before the great Inca Empire was formed, wandering hunters lived in both North and South America. They had come to the Americas over a natural bridge of land between present-day Alaska and Asia. These early people were following the herds of wild animals that provided them with meat for food, skins for clothing, and bones for making simple tools.

Gradually some of the hunters discovered that seeds grew into plants and that plants could be cultivated. As a result of this discovery some of the Indians settled down to farming. Now that

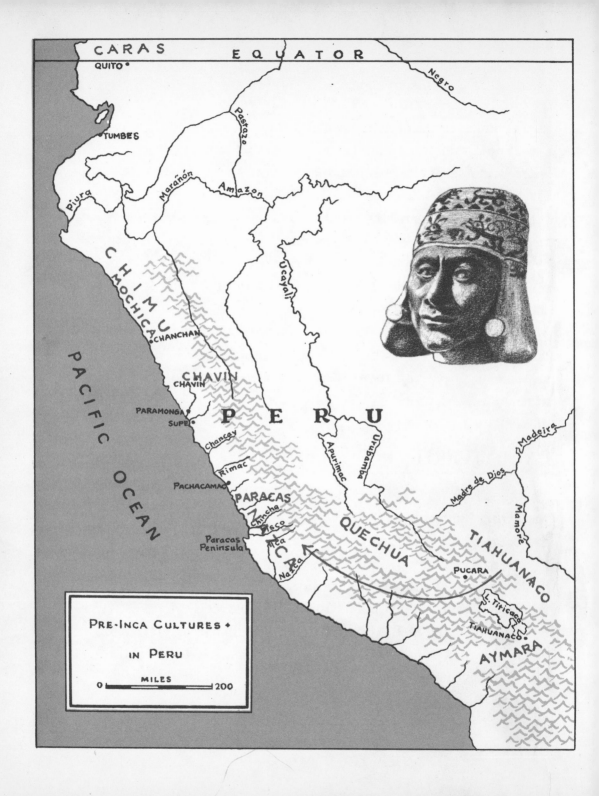

CARAS

EQUATOR

QUITO

Negro

TUMBES

Pastaza

Piura

Marañón

Amazon

C H I M U

MOCHICA

CHANCHAN

Ucayali

CHAVIN

CHAVIN

PARAMONGA

SUPE

P E R U

Chancay

Apurímac

Urubamba

Madeira

PACIFIC OCEAN

Rimac

PACHACAMAC

PARACAS

Chincha

Madre de Dios

Pisco

Ica

QUECHUA

TIAHUANACO

Mamoré

Paracas
Peninsula

Nazca

PUCARA

L. Titicaca

TIAHUANACO

AYMARA

PRE-INCA CULTURES ✦

IN PERU

MILES

0          200

they had learned to sow seed and to cultivate and harvest plants, life became easier and more certain for them.

The most important plant grown in the Americas was maize, or Indian corn. The great "maize kingdoms" were those of the Aztecs of the Valley of Mexico, the Maya of Guatemala and the Yucatán Peninsula, and the Incas of Peru. Scientists say that the maize plant probably originated in Central America as long ago as 2500 B.C. The cultivation of corn slowly spread down and along the west coast of South America.

Along the coast of Peru small farming communities had sprung up, followed by villages. When maize became a crop, these communities developed more rapidly than before. In time, they banded together and were probably governed by priest-rulers. The simple farmers and fishermen prayed to the earth, the sun, the moon, the stars, the sea, and the rivers, and to such animals as the puma. Gradually the Indians became skilled at pottery making, weaving, and other handicrafts.

Some of the most important pre-Inca civilizations were the Chavín, in the north Peruvian highlands and along the coast; the Paracas, located south of modern Lima; the Nazca, south of the Paracas; the Mochica, in the area around the Moche River valley on the north coast of Peru; and the Tiahuanaco, centered around Lake Titicaca, which lies partly in present-day Bolivia. Because scholars do not know the real names of most pre-Inca peoples they have called many of them after the river valleys, the peninsulas, or other geographical sites where they lived.

*The people of Paracas were master weavers. This textile shows a human with the head of a cat.*

The ruins of the city of Chavín de Huántar, in a narrow valley of the Andes, show the people there as clever architects and artists. In their fine stone carving, pottery, textiles, and metalwork they pictured their fierce, catlike god. The Chavín civilization began around 350 B.C. and lasted for about six hundred years.

The Paracas culture, lasting from about 400 B.C. to A.D. 400, is famous for two things: mummies and weaving. Although we know almost nothing of the Paracas people — not even their real name — we still have many of their colorful, beautifully woven textiles, which are some of the finest ever found in the Americas.

The Paracas Indians prepared their dead with great care. They tied them in a sitting position, then wrapped them in lengths of

8

woven cloth. Along with the wrappings they placed many pieces of clothing: poncho shirts, cloaks, caps, and breechcloths. The bundles thus formed were placed in underground chambers and covered with logs and sand. Some of these chambers contained not just one, but scores of mummy bundles buried one on top of another. Coastal Peru's hot sun raises the temperature in these underground tombs to that of an oven. The intense heat has dried everything and has preserved the cloth wrappings. The beautifully colored ponchos, breechcloths, cloaks, and caps found there today were plainly created by a highly civilized people.

Between A.D. 400 and 1000 the Mochica people appeared on the coast. These people built cities, roads, irrigation systems, and canals and aqueducts, and they maintained armies. They used mass-production methods to produce weaving and perhaps their other handicrafts. Their pottery, often made in molds, is so lively and realistic that it plainly tells the story of the Mochica daily life to us today.

*The Paracas people buried their dead sitting in bundles of beautifully woven fabrics. Some of these graves were lined with stones and were similar to the Indians' houses.*

The great Temple of the Sun and Temple of the Moon near present-day Trujillo were built by the Mochica people. Their society was based on a class system, with priests, warriors, and nobles at the top, and with farmers and fishermen below them. The Mochica people were war-minded. They conquered several important coastal valleys.

To the south of the Paracas Peninsula was the Nazca civilization. The Nazca people are somewhat of a mystery. They do not seem to have been interested in building great centers or in conquering other tribes. Archeologists have discovered no Nazca fortifications and they have found only one city, thought to be the capital. The Nazca people were craftsmen. Their weaving was nearly as fine as the Paracas weaving. Nazca pottery was thinner than the Paracas ware and was painted in many beautiful colors. The Nazca designs pictured birds, fish, fruits, and strange mythological demons.

Today the Nazca region is also known for the mysterious lines and geometrical figures these people cut out of the earth. The patterns, which they made by scraping away the earth's stony brown crust and revealing the yellow sand beneath, can only be seen from an airplane. Some of the lines are as long as five miles. We can only guess what these lines and patterns, now nearly fifteen hundred years old, may mean. Some scholars think they were used to make astronomical observations as a basis for a calendar.

Some time around A.D. 1000, one vigorous group of people from the southern highlands began to influence the civilizations along the coast. The invaders' art style seems to have spread suddenly. It

10

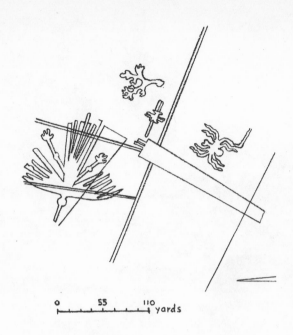

*Airview of lines dug in the sand by the Nazca people.*

0    55    110 yards

is now called the Tiahuanacan style. It brought to the coast the religion of the "weeping god," who was pictured with "tear bands" around his eyes.

The ceremonial center of the Tiahuanacan culture was the bleak *altiplano*, or "high plain," of Bolivia, at an elevation of nearly three miles. On this cold, dreary plain the ruins of Tiahuanaco can still be seen. There are four large groups of structures and several smaller ones. At one time Tiahuanaco contained a fortress built on a step-sided pyramid. It is called the Acapana. To the north of it is a huge rectangular structure called the Calasasaya. This contained a huge inner court, and a great doorway now known as the Gate-

11

*The Gateway at Tiahuanaco, often called the Gateway of the Sun, is cut out of a block of lava 12½ by 10 feet. The figure over the doorway is thought to be the Creator God, Viracocha. The halo around his head depicts condor heads. Because a stream of tears seems to come from his eyes he is often called the Weeping God.*

way of the Sun. The Puma Puncu, or Lion's Gate, is another platform structure of huge stones, some of which weigh as much as one hundred tons. Here are the remains of cutout stone seats, staircases, statues, and altars. An area called the Palacio still has many finished stone blocks and a painted staircase.

For some reason the Tiahuanacan style was short-lived in the coastal lands. Even so, it left its mark. For many years after its influence had lessened, coastal pottery and weaving still depicted the weeping god, pumas, condors, and snakes in the Tiahuanacan way. Today the great stones of Tiahuanaco, standing silently on the windswept *altiplano*, remain as a vivid memorial to this culture from which the Incas took many ideas.

When the Tiahuanacan influence began to fade, many small nations again sprang up along the coast of Peru. Archeologists call this time the City-Builder Period. Of the coastal nations, the Chimu, dating approximately from A.D. 1000 to 1466, is the best known. The Chimu Kingdom was an outgrowth of the Mochica Empire and included about six hundred miles of coast, extending

*This monolithic stone statue was found at Tiahuanaco, near Lake Titicaca, by the famous archeologist Wendell C. Bennett.*

*The* chullpas, *or burial towers, were built by an unknown people following the Tiahuanaco civilization. Some are round, some square, but all contained the bodies of dead chieftains.*

roughly from present-day Lima to Ecuador. Chanchan was the capital.

This carefully planned city of six square miles contained enormous pyramids, walls as high as forty feet, and a maze of sheltered streets, houses, terraces, and cemeteries. Chanchan's engineers constructed irrigation systems and huge stone-lined reservoirs to hold precious river water for the farmers' fields. The city was built of large adobe bricks — blocks of sun-dried mud. Adobe will last for centuries in a dry, sunny climate, but Chanchan is in ruins today because of freak rainstorms which have washed away most of the adobe.

One of the noticeable details of Chimu cities, and of others built during the same period, is the designs formed in the clay of many of the walls. These small, intricate designs — many of them geometrical or of birds and fishes — were arranged in textile-like patterns which were repeated over and over again.

Only people with a strong central government could have built such grand cities as Chanchan. It would have taken a strong government to organize the necessary large labor forces and to direct their activities.

While the kingdoms of the coast were thriving, a handful of Indians in and around Cuzco were beginning to gather strength. In less than one hundred years they would build an empire and would rule over all the coastal and highland peoples.

*Chanchan was the capital city of the powerful Chimu people. The ruins shown above are in the Moche Valley, near the modern city of Trujillo. The inset shows the type of decoration the Chimu "printed" on their walls over and over again.*

*According to Inca mythology, Viracocha, Lord of Beginnings, first appeared here, at Lake Titicaca, in the bleak* altiplano *section of Peru and Bolivia. The boats in the foreground are made today of totora reeds, just as they were in pre-Inca times.*

## THE COMING OF THE INCAS

There are many myths and legends about the beginnings of the Inca people. It is said that Ticci Viracocha (TI-ki Wi-ra-co-cha), Lord of the Beginnings, came forth from the waters of Lake Titicaca and that he created heaven and earth. Then he made a race of men, but when they quarreled among themselves, Viracocha turned them into stones. Supposedly these are the same great stones

16

found at Tiahuanaco. Some time later, Viracocha again came out of the lake and put the sun and moon in the heavens. This time he created a new race, the Incas, and set a ruler over them.

Another myth about Viracocha tells us that this Supreme Being was a god who went among all the tribes, teaching the people how to cultivate plants, organize their governments, and lead good lives. He taught them languages, customs, and even dances. Viracocha is pictured as a gigantic man dressed in long white robes and with a great beard. It is said that when Viracocha finished his teachings he came to the coast of Ecuador. There he held out his robes and was borne across the tops of the waves, never to be seen again.

Still another legend tells of four brothers and four sisters who lived on an island in Lake Titicaca. Viracocha appeared before them, saying that they would one day conquer many lands. The

*Manco Capac, the first Lord Inca. (Redrawn from Poma de Ayala.)*

brothers set out to found an empire. For a long time they lived in a cave, but when the oldest brother proved troublesome the other three walled him up in the cave. Later, a second brother was turned to stone, and a third was changed into a stone field-guardian. Only one brother, Manco Capac, the founder of the Inca people, was left.

A fourth legend tells that the Sun God created Manco Capac and his sister on the Isle of the Sun in Lake Titicaca. Arming Manco Capac with a golden staff, the Sun God instructed him and his sister to search for a homeland. Where the staff of gold was thrown down and sank out of sight, there would be their dwelling place. The couple wandered northward until they came to the beautiful valley of Cuzco. The golden rod was cast down and disappeared into the ground. Cuzco, capital of the Incas, was thus founded in 1250.

At first, Cuzco was only a handful of stone huts with thatched roofs. Contrary to the heroic Inca legends, Indians were already living in this village when the Incas came. The Incas were probably a small tribe who spoke a language later called Quechua.

It is said that Manco Capac and his wife, whose name was Mama Ocllo, built a house in Cuzco on the site of the Temple of the Sun, or Coricancha, which later became the most magnificent, most holy spot in all the realm. Standing near the meeting of two streams, Coricancha included the Temple of the Sun, and shrines to the moon, Venus, the stars, the lightning, and the rainbow. On the wall of the main sanctuary — dedicated to the sun, or Inti — was an enormous golden disk. The rays of the morning sun fell on

18

*Coricancha, in Cuzco. According to Cieza de León, this famous shrine contained a golden garden in which stood some twenty full-sized llamas and shepherds, made of solid gold.*

this disk, and it lighted up the whole shrine. The Temple of the Moon contained a similar disk of silver.

The *Villac Uma* (WIL-lac oo-ma), or high priest, lived at Coricancha. Only members of the ruling family and a few very important priests could enter its sacred walls.

The Coricancha shrines were grouped around an enclosure. According to Cieza de León and other Spanish writers, this enclosure contained a fountain of gold and an artificial garden of cornstalks whose ears were made of solid gold. The walls of the enclosure were said to be plated in gold, and mingled with the grass thatching

19

of the enclosure's roof were golden straws, which gleamed in the sun.

Today the church and monastery of Santo Domingo stand in Cuzco on what is left of the beautifully cut, gray stones of Coricancha. Inside Santo Domingo work is being done to uncover the original Inca walls of the building.

Ancient Cuzco, capital of the Incas, was divided into two parts: lower Cuzco — or Hurin — and upper Cuzco — or Hanan. Besides Coricancha, lower Cuzco included the palaces of the rulers and the homes of the nobles. Situated on narrow streets were many houses of finely cut, polished, and fitted stone. Upper Cuzco contained the peasants' houses, which were of poorer workmanship than the homes in Lower Cuzco.

Four main roads led from the capital. At first they merely went short distances, to the small villages of hostile tribes. In the early years of the Incas, from about 1250 to 1438, the ambitious "Children of the Sun" waged constant warfare on their neighbors. But finally, in the time of the ninth ruler, Pachacuti, the roads led long distances to the four quarters of the Inca realm. Though not exactly accurate by the compass, these quarters were called the Collasuyu, or southeastern quarter; the Antisuyu, or northeastern quarter; the Chinchasuyu, or northwestern quarter; and the Cuntisuyu, or southwestern quarter. These four quarters account for the Incas' name for their empire: Tahuantinsuyu, or "Land of the Four Quarters."

With Pachacuti the real history of Tahuantinsuyu, the Inca Empire, began.

# THE LORD INCA AND HIS GOVERNMENT

The Lord Inca was the head of the empire and of the imperial court at Cuzco. He had many wives — often several hundred — but his one true wife was the queen, called the *coya*. The Inca chose a successor from among his sons. The boy was usually the most promising son of the *coya*. He became heir to the throne. A young prince was probably taught by his parents because, of course, no ordinary person could teach a living god. The boy was expected to endure all the physical hardships that the sons of nobles were trained to suffer, however. He probably was given even sterner tests because of his high rank.

*This gold crown is thought to have belonged to Huayna Capac, the last great Inca. It was found in his palace, Tumibamba.*

When the Inca died, the prince fasted for three days in a house built especially for the occasion. Then he was adorned with the sign of royalty — a fringe of small gold tubes from which dangled red tassels. This fringe hung down over his forehead.

A great feast followed the adornment of the new Inca. It lasted for days. A palace was built for the new ruler because the former palace now contained his father's mummy and was sealed up forever. Often the former Inca's servants and favorite wives volunteered to die too, so that they could accompany their lord.

The Inca's palace had walls that were plated with sheets of gold and silver. One room contained the throne, probably a low, red wooden stool covered with a beautiful cloth. Garcilaso de la Vega writes, however, that this stool was of solid gold and that it was placed on a raised platform of gold. Aside from this stool there was very little furniture in the palace.

The Lord Inca carried a star-headed war club made of gold. His clothing was similar to that of common men, but was woven of fine vicuña wool and was never worn more than once. In his earlobes the Inca wore huge golden earplugs decorated with jewels. He ate and drank from gold and silver plates and cups held by women from his household. Whatever was left over from the meal was placed with each day's clothing, to be saved and ceremonially burned once a year. The Inca slept on the floor on a quilted cotton mattress, under blankets of fine wool.

The Lord Inca rarely walked. He was carried from place to place on a royal litter plated with gold and shaded by a canopy of

*The Inca and his* coya *were usually carried in a litter borne by servants. The litter was often plated with gold and studded with jewels. (Redrawn from Poma de Ayala.)*

gold, inlaid with jewels. The litter was carried on the shoulders of men from the province of Rucana. Two or three hundred litter bearers went along to prepare the way ahead and to relieve bearers who became tired.

Many tribes provided special services to the Lord Inca. The Canari furnished men to be his bodyguards. The Chumpivilca furnished court dancers or jesters. These services were part of the tax every subject must pay.

The Inca chose his administrators from among the nobles of the royal family. They dressed like their lord. Their clothing was not as fine, however, and their earplugs were somewhat smaller, although the slits in their earlobes were still large enough to pass an

*An ear ornament.*

egg through. (When the Spanish first saw these men they called them *orejones,* or "big ears.") Nobles were permitted to use litters and carry parasols — two signs of their aristocracy.

The nobles of royal blood had more power than another order of nobles called *curacas* (koo-RA-kas). *Curacas* were often the leaders of conquered tribes or territories and were appointed because of their ability. A *curaca* of the lowest rank had charge of only one hundred men, while a high-ranking *curaca* was the chief of ten thousand men. Their posts were inherited, while those of the Inca's governors and relatives were not.

The life of the common people during empire days was strictly controlled by the Inca and the two noble classes. Each family belonged to a group called an *ayllu* (I-loo). The *ayllu* made up a number of related families living together in a small area and sharing everything: land, crops, and animals. *Ayllus* were the foundation of the Incas' social and economic life.

The Inca people were divided into age groups. The kind and amount of work done by each age group was clearly stated. For example, a *rocto macho* was a man between the ages of eighty and one hundred who was not expected to do anything but keep rabbits and ducks and weave ropes.

All able-bodied men between the ages of twenty-five and fifty were called *purics* (POO-riks). They were divided into groups of

*Tambomachay, often called the Inca's Bath, is about four miles from Cuzco.*

ten, who obeyed a work leader, who in turn obeyed a foreman. Each foreman controlled ten work leaders. Ten foremen had a supervisor who was generally the head of the village. Jumping each time by tens, the group finally reached ten thousand workers, who were commanded by a *tucui-rucuc* (too-koo-i roo-kook), or "he who sees all." This man answered to the governor of the province. The governor, ruling many such chiefs, reported to the *Apo Capac* (His Excellency), head of one of the quarters of the empire. The *Apo Capac*, in turn, served the Lord Inca.

All farmland was divided three ways: one part for the government; one part for the support of the priests and religion; one part for the community. Each season all the villagers worked the fields of the gods first. Next they worked the Inca's lands. Lastly each of them worked his share of the community fields. In the highlands, herds of llamas and alpacas were also divided three ways.

Each year a government overseer redivided the land of the peasants according to their needs. A new baby in the family brought more land, whereas the marriage of a son took some away. A newly married couple received one *topo* (too-poo) of land — a strip about 150 feet by 300 feet. Thereafter an extra strip was given for a son and one-half a strip for a daughter. The size of the lands belonging to the religious authorities and to the state was not changed from year to year.

The sacred fields of the gods were never crossed by workers without their repeating certain prayers. At sowing and harvest times everyone came out to work the soil. Even the Lord Inca

*This* chasqui *is shown blowing a horn made from a conch shell, to signal his arrival to the next runner. (Redrawn from Poma de Ayala.)*

arrived with a golden spade and began the ceremony by turning over the first piece of sod. Nobles and other officials did the same, but their work was merely a token. They soon stopped, leaving the peasants to carry on.

The Incas never developed a money system. The people paid their taxes by working for the government. This tax service was called *mit'a* (MEE-ta). *Mit'a* required people to work a certain amount of time on state projects: building roads; working in gold and silver mines; constructing bridges; serving in the army; providing *chasquis* (CHAZ-kees), or runners, who carried messages over the royal roads; or doing other public work.

Artists, craftsmen, and other skilled workers were not required

*The* quipu *was a series of knotted strings of different colors which were tied to a main rope. The boxlike divisions at the left probably show the system of counting used by the Incas. Numbers one to nine were recorded at the ends of the strings; the tens, hundreds, and thousands were recorded in that order, closer to the base cord. (Redrawn from Poma de Ayala.)*

to work in the fields or serve a work tax as they were government employees and were supported by the state.

To count all his people and keep track of what they produced, the Lord Inca employed many accountants, or *quipucamayocs* (kee-poo-kam-a-yoks). The *quipu* (kee-poo) was the Inca counting device. It was a series of knotted strings of various colors and thicknesses. By making knots on the *quipu*, a *quipucamayoc* could record how many people lived in a certain province or how much corn was stored away or many other things. The *quipu* was based on the decimal system, counting in units of ten, and was a kind of record, though the Incas never discovered true writing.

28

When the Lord Inca set out to conquer a tribe or country, word was sent out to the far corners of his realm. Able-bodied men were recruited. Since they had been trained in warfare from boyhood and brought their own weapons with them, it was not hard to form a well-disciplined army quickly.

Weapons were simple. The bola consisted of a number of stones, each tied to a thong. All the thongs were then tied together. When the bola was thrown, the thongs wrapped themselves around the victim's legs, thus stopping his flight. For hand-to-hand combat the Incas had stone-headed clubs, battle-axes, spears, and double-edged swords. They used slings for hurling rocks. A sling was made of braided or woven wool or fiber and was often six feet long. It had a wide section in the middle for holding a small rock. Gripping the two ends of the sling, the soldier whirled it over his head until it gained speed and energy. Then he released one end, sending the rock with great force at his enemy.

*(A) Star-headed mace for close-in fighting; (B) sling, with rock, for distance fighting; (C) war ax, and (D) rope mace, both of the latter used for infighting. (Not drawn to scale.)*

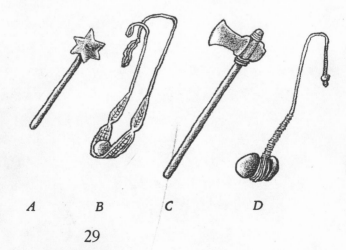

A     B     C     D

Weapons, except for those that threw rocks, were usually made of stone or fire-hardened wood, or were tipped with copper or bronze. For protection the Incas wore heavily quilted cotton shirts and used wooden slats to protect their backs. They also carried round or square shields made of wood or toughened deer hide. These shields were painted with geometric designs in bright colors. In addition, when the men were attacking fortified places, a great sheet of cloth was held in front of them. It could protect about one hundred men from slingstones.

The assembled army must have been a colorful sight, for all the *purics* from each district wore the kind of helmet special to their group. The helmets were made of wood or strands of woven cane.

The Incas were accustomed to war, and their captains were clever leaders. They used such tricks as ambushing, setting grass fires, and leaving the battle in apparent defeat only to return at dawn and catch their opponents off guard.

The Inca's army marched over royal roads to the beat of drums and the music of flutes and trumpets. *Purics* used the royal roads only during wartime, because traveling was strictly forbidden for the common man. Ordinarily he must stay with his land and his *ayllu*.

One reason Inca armies were so successful was that government storehouses holding food were placed along the royal roads only a day's march apart. Soldiers were not allowed to leave the highway and forage the countryside.

Before actually fighting a battle the Incas sent envoys to their enemies, inviting them to join the empire without bloodshed. Often news of the many benefits enjoyed by the Inca people arrived ahead of the Inca's army. Many enemy leaders were persuaded, and willingly agreed to Inca rule. Thereby they avoided battle. Others realized that the Inca commanded a stronger army, and they gave in without a struggle. Those nations who fought and lost were usually forgiven, although sometimes their rulers were brought back to Cuzco. There they were publicly trod on by the Inca, or sometimes they were put to death and their skulls were made into drinking cups.

Inca soldiers were garrisoned in a defeated country, and Inca governors were sent in to organize the people. A census was taken, the area was divided into *ayllus*, and the sons of royal and noble families were sent back to Cuzco to be educated. If tribes were stubborn about learning the Inca ways, their people were taken in large groups — or even in whole villages — and sent to the Inca homeland. They were replaced in the conquered land by loyal Inca subjects called *mitimaes* (mit-i-MAH-ays). The *mitimaes* set a good example for the newly conquered people. They instructed the new subjects in the Inca religion and taught them the Quechua language. *Mitimaes* received special favors for their work.

The gods of newly conquered people were not usually forbidden. They became minor gods of the Inca religion. But *Inti,* or sun worship, was expected of new citizens.

The Incas had a special talent: they were able to make one empire out of many different peoples from many different tribes with

*The semicircular Temple of the Sun, at Machu Picchu.*

many different backgrounds. The Incas could do this because their system of government was geared for conquering new lands and for making subjects of the captive peoples.

Today we would say that the victorious Incas brainwashed those they overcame. The Incas' story was that the conquered land had been populated by wretched savages before they arrived; that there had been no cities, no houses, no roads. Gradually, over the years, the tribes who had been subdued by these vigorous highlanders forgot their own history and could only remember and believe the Incas' story. In addition, the Incas told the people certain legends that seemed to prove that they, the Incas, were indeed superior people.

Under Inca law the two greatest crimes, punishable by death, were disobedience to the Lord Inca, and treason. There was also a death penalty for stealing. Since nearly everything, except for a few personal belongings, was owned by the state, stealing was an offense against the government. Criminal cases were argued before Inca officials as judges. If a thief could convince these judges that he stole from need, they gave a severe punishment to the authority who had overlooked this need. They considered that this authority had not done his job properly.

Laziness was considered a form of stealing because it robbed the Inca of the working time due him. Laziness was first punished by public rebuke. If the offender still did not work, he was stoned. Finally, if he had not learned his lesson, he was killed.

There was really no need to steal during Inca times, for the state saw to it that everyone shared equally. There was no poverty. When crops failed — as they sometimes did — the Inca's storehouses were opened to the public, and food and clothing were divided equally among the people. The *purics* did not grumble about working the Inca's fields because they knew that during hard times he would take care of his subjects.

## THE INCA PEOPLE

The Inca people were highlanders who lived in the Andes Mountains. Today the Indians in this area still live and look much like their ancestors did five hundred years ago.

Highland Indians are short in stature. The men average 5 feet, 3 inches, in height. The women average 4 feet, 10 inches. The Indians' skin ranges from coppery to chestnut brown in color. Their eyes are dark. They have high cheekbones and straight black hair. As is true of many Indian races, Inca men had so little hair on their faces that they did not shave, but pulled out the hair with tweezers. In the highlands the Indians have developed barrel-shaped chests by means of which they can take in more air than usual with every breath. This helps make up for the lack of oxygen in the atmosphere at such high altitudes. Cuzco is almost 12,000 feet above sea level, and the empire extended to areas that were over 16,000 feet in altitude.

Highland Indians have great strength and stamina. Without

*These ruins at Pisac crown a mountain spur, the sides of which are terraced. Pisac was an important city during Inca times.*

ever stopping to catch their breath they can walk for miles with a hundred-pound load strapped to their backs.

During empire days the dress of the common people was simple. Men wore breechcloths which were held around the waist by a woolen belt. They also wore sleeveless tunics — straight, shirtlike garments that reached to the knees. A cloak, often woven of alpaca wool, was added on cold days and was also used as a blanket at night. No man set off for the day without wearing a little pouch under his cloak. In this small bag he kept his personal possessions, including magical charms and sometimes coca leaves for chewing.

The clothing of the common people was woven of fairly coarse textiles — wool from the highlands, and cotton from the coast. The amount of colorful decoration woven into the garments depended on a man's importance in his community.

Women wore sacklike dresses which reached to their ankles. A dress was secured over each shoulder by metal pins, and was held in at the waist by a long, wide belt. Women also wore woolen cloaks for warmth. Men and women alike wore sandals or went barefoot, just as Peruvian highlanders do today.

One tribesman could tell another by the way his hair was arranged. The Lord Inca decreed that each tribe or province must keep its individual hairstyle, with whatever combs, ribbons, or other ornaments were customary. Mostly, though, the men cut their hair in bangs. The Inca also ruled that the members of the tribe must wear distinctive headgear.

Day-to-day life was simple and hard. The members of a house-

36

*Many Inca terraces are still in use in Peru. These overlook the beautiful valley of Pisac.*

hold rose early and ate a meal sometimes made up of leftovers from the day before. The men drank a malt beverage, or beer, now called *chicha*, then they left for the fields.

Highland farmers often grew their crops on terraces that were like steps on the sides of the mountains. By using these terraces they put every possible bit of good soil to use.

Highland crops included corn, beans, potatoes, squashes, peppers, tobacco, quinoa, and oca. Quinoa is a plant which produces many

37

tiny seeds. These were boiled like rice, or ground into a meal and made into cakes. The underground tubers of the oca were cooked until they made a thick, nourishing porridge.

At very high altitudes in the highlands — over 11,500 or 12,000 feet — only potatoes, quinoa, oca, and a few little-known plants can grow. On these grassy, windswept plateaus the Indians were not mainly farmers, but were herders of llamas and alpacas.

Potatoes were the Indians' main food here. The potatoes were preserved by squeezing the water out of them after they had been left to freeze and thaw many times. After being dried in the sun, this food was called *chuñu* (CHOO-nyoo).

Along the coast of Peru and in warm, protected valleys the plants grown were corn, cotton, beans, squashes, tomatoes, many tropical fruits, cacao (or chocolate), and peanuts.

Some time after midday the farming families returned from the fields for a meal, usually a soup or stew of some kind. At times it was made of boiled corn and chili peppers, cooked with herbs. Strips of sun-dried llama meat, called *charqui* (CHAR-kee), were boiled with *chuñu* and other vegetables to make a thick soup called *locro*. Guinea pigs or ducks were served as meat. In addition, corn was ground and made into dough. This was sometimes cooked as dumplings in the stew. At other times it was dropped into hot ashes and baked. Corn was also eaten on the cob, and popcorn was thought to be a great treat.

When members of the family had finished working in the field for the day they sometimes had an evening meal of soup. In

38

the waning daylight hours the men repaired their tools, and the women made *chicha* beer, often from corn. First they put the corn in their mouths and chewed it. Then they spat it into a jar of warm water. The mixture was allowed to stand until it fermented because of the saliva mixed with it in chewing. This same process, using quinoa or oca, was followed at higher altitudes where corn could not grow.

The women's work was never done. In addition to cooking, keeping house, grinding corn, working in the fields and taking a turn at guarding them at night, and raising children, the women spun thread and wove clothing for their families.

The houses were small and rectangular, usually made either of fieldstone held together with mud, or else of blocks of adobe. The roofs were thatched with grass. There were seldom any windows and there was only one low doorway. The "door" was often nothing more than a stick or woolen curtain that barred the way. Cooking was frequently done out of doors over a fire ringed by low stones. If the cooking was done inside on a stone or clay fireplace, the smoke escaped through the thatched roof. The floor was made of pounded-down earth upon which the Indians laid their blankets when it was time to sleep. Animals, including guinea pigs, scurried in and out of the hut. On the walls were pegs for clothing, and slots or niches for idols.

At plantingtime, following a festival, the ground was broken with a wooden spade, or "foot plow," called a *taclla*. The men formed lines and dug, working backward, while the women came

*Plowing the fields. Rows of men worked backward while the women broke clumps of earth with their hands. A foreman supervised the work. (Redrawn from Poma de Ayala.)*

after, on their knees, breaking each clod of earth into loose soil. Next, the men made holes in the ground with a planting stick. Again the women followed, dropping grains of corn into the holes. According to custom the women did the sowing because seeds would not come up otherwise. Other farming tools included a hoe and a doughnut-shaped stone attached to a handle, which was used for breaking up clods of earth.

Because crops depend on water, the rainy season was anxiously awaited. If rain failed to come, the people dressed in mourning clothes and walked, weeping, through the villages. Often they tied up black llamas or dogs so that they cried piteously from hunger

40

*These present-day llamas walk by Inca walls still standing in Cuzco.*

and thirst. The people thought these cries would soften the hearts of the gods so that they would send rain.

The llama and alpaca herds were very important to the highland Incas. These animals supplied wool for clothing, and the llamas provided meat, and hides which were used as floor coverings. Llamas and alpacas are relatives of the camel and share many of his disagreeable habits. They are stubborn, and spit when angry. Llamas can travel for miles without water. No one rides them because they balk at carrying a person's weight, but they can transport loads of about one hundred pounds. There were no other pack animals in Peru until the Spaniards brought horses from Europe.

The wild guanaco (hwan-A-co) and the vicuña (vi-KYU-nya) were two other relatives of the camel. They were captured in round-ups decreed by the Lord Inca. Thousands of Indians gathered in a great circle around the animals. Gradually the circle grew smaller and smaller until the *purics* could hold hands. Cieza de León says that as many as forty thousand guanacos and vicuñas were often trapped within a circle. The guanacos were killed for meat, but the vicuñas were freed after being sheared of their fine wool. The guanaco meat was dried and divided among the people, but vicuña wool was reserved for the use of the Inca and his blood relatives.

Every one of the common men was expected to marry. If a man did not choose a wife from his own village by the time he was twenty, the state picked one for him. In some areas the marriage ceremony consisted of nothing more than a girl's placing her left foot in a woolen slipper held by her husband-to-be. This act was followed by a great feast with much drinking and dancing. Sometimes the girl gave the groom a fine woolen tunic, a headband, and a special metal ornament, all of which he put on. With the marriage came a *topo* of land. When the couple had children they were given more land.

Soon after a baby was born he was tied onto a kind of portable wooden crib which could be slung over his mother's back or could be stood on the floor. A child stayed in this cradle until he could walk.

Inca children learned by imitating their fathers and mothers. Boys learned farming and llama herding. Girls learned weaving, cooking, and other household duties. The only schools were for the nobility. When young boys came of age in their early teens, a festival was held in the community. Girls, on the other hand, were treated to a private family celebration. At their celebrations both boys and girls were given new names and new clothes. A person had several names during his lifetime. He had a name given at birth, a nickname, and later the name he was given at the coming-of-age ceremony.

During the Inca times there was probably very little time for fun and games, though archeologists have found objects like dice, and balls, tops, and dolls, as well.

*An Inca doll, found near the coast of Peru.*

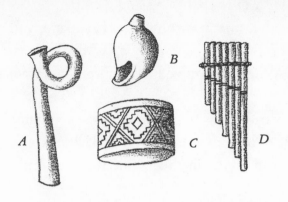

*Inca musical instruments. (A) A horn; (B) a conch-shell flute; (C) a tambour; (D) panpipes.*

Every month a religious festival was held. The names of the twelve Inca months describe for us these celebrations. For example, *Capac Raimi*, held in December, means "magnificent festival"; *Pauca Huaray*, held in March, means "earth ripening"; *Inti Raimi*, held in June, means "festival of the sun."

At the twelve monthly festivals the people danced, joined in sports such as footraces, sang, and played musical instruments. The musical instruments included tambourines, bells, drums made from a hollow log with a tight deerskin cover, trumpets made from seashells or baked clay, flutes made from the bones of animals, and panpipes made of reeds or clay.

Dancing made use of a great deal of pantomime. For instance, in dancing, farmers acted out their daily chores, or soldiers went through the motions of a battle to the rhythm of the music. Sometimes festivals lasted as long as a week. When they were over, the people returned to their fields and herds.

# RELIGION, SUPERSTITION, AND MEDICINE

The ancient Peruvian people were deeply religious and superstitious. The supreme Inca god was the Creator, or Viracocha, Lord of Beginnings. Next to him came Inti, the Sun God. Then came the gods and goddesses of thunder, the earth, the moon, Venus, the stars, the sea, and the rainbow, among others. The Thunder God was really a weather, or rain, god. In Inca designs his sister is often shown holding a jar of water. It was believed that when the Thunder God wished rain to fall he broke the jar with his slingshot. The thunderclap was said to be the crack of the slingshot. The rainwater was believed to come from the Milky Way, thought to be a river in the skies.

The Lord Inca was considered to be the "son of the sun," and therefore a god, too. Usually his favorite brother or some other

*The sacred rock of Kenko ("twisted channels") stands in a stone-lined amphitheater near Cuzco. Just beyond the rock is a series of underground passageways which contain wall carvings of animal figures, and altars which were probably used during sacrifices.*

*These buildings without roofs hang on the edge of a sheer cliff opposite the fortress of Ollantaytambo. They are called the House of the Nuestas ("Chosen Women").*

favorite close relative became the high priest, or *Villac Umu*, and officiated at all great festivals. There were many lesser priests who helped sacrifice animals (and sometimes children) to the gods. They also heard confessions, interpreted oracles, or cured sick people.

Although there were temples to the sun in nearly every Inca city, these were not churches. Religious ceremonies were held out of doors. Near the sun temples were buildings for "Chosen Women," and "Virgins of the Sun." Each year, government officials visited the villages in search of the prettiest and most talented ten-year-old girls. These were sent to Cuzco, where they were especially trained.

They were known as Chosen Women, and some of them served as wives to the nobility or were sent to the Lord Inca's household. Others became Virgins of the Sun. They were assigned to the various sun temples. They wove the garments of the priests and the ceremonial cloths, and helped the priests in other ways.

Besides the official gods, the common people worshiped *huacas* (WAK-as), or sacred shrines. Cuzco was a *huaca*; Pachacamac on the coast of Peru, with its famous oracle, was also a *huaca*. People made pilgrimages to these two sacred places. In addition, stones, springs, mountains, caves, tombs, temples, palaces, and many other objects were *huacas*. Each was believed to be the home of a spirit who must be kept in good humor. A special type of *huaca* was an *apachita* (a-pach-EE-ta), a pile of rocks at a dangerous turn in the road. Here travelers prayed for safety on their journey and then cast a stone, a bit of old cloth, or something else onto the *apachita*.

Soothsayers or diviners were members of the priest class, and interpreted signs and omens. Soothsaying was often done by casting pebbles or corn on the ground or by watching what turn a snake took or how llama fat burned in a fire. Twitching eyelids, the howl of a dog, or a fire that suddenly flared up — all had special meaning to diviners and to common people alike.

The Incas believed that sickness was usually caused by sorcery or the ill will of other people, or by the gods, who had been angered. Illness, then, was treated by magic and by religion. Sometimes a medicine man, or sorcerer, was supposed to "remove" the troublesome object from the patient's body, and so to cure him. To

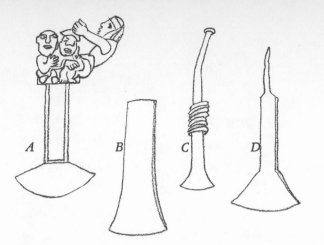

(A) A ceremonial knife with a decoration showing how a trepanning operation was done. (B and C) Bronze scalpels. (D) A knife used for cutting bone.

do this, the medicine man waved his hand over the afflicted part. Soon there appeared in his hand a small object such as a pin or stone, which was supposed to have caused the trouble. The patient was thus made well. Curing was accompanied by prayers, by offerings to the gods, and sometimes by a ceremonial washing of the patient in a nearby stream.

Despite all this belief in sorcery and magic the Incas understood a good deal about medicine and surgery. Extracts from various plants were used in treatment: cocaine, from the coca plant, used to relieve pain; belladonna, used for the eyes; and tobacco, used as snuff. Resin from a certain tree healed wounds.

It is known that the ancient Peruvians could perform an operation on the skull called trepanning. When a warrior received a severe blow on the head he was probably given coca (cocaine) or some other drug to deaden the pain. The surgeon then operated to remove the shattered pieces of bone that pressed on the brain. Many surgical instruments have been found in Peruvian graves: scalpels, knives, needles for stitching up wounds, and pincers. Tourniquets, used to stem the flow of blood, and bandages have also been found.

48

# THE INCAS' ACHIEVEMENTS

The Incas' efficient system of government was probably their greatest achievement, but next to this came the famous Inca roads and buildings. At the height of the empire the roads covered nearly ten thousand miles. A coastal highway extended for 2,520 miles from Tumbes in the north to Arequipa — almost to present-day Chile — in the south. Some authorities say that this road continued for hundreds of miles into Chile. In addition, high in the Andes was a royal road that ran for 3,250 miles up and down the spiny back of South America. Other roads crisscrossed back and forth between these two great highways. Each highway was named for the Lord Inca in whose reign it had been built.

The Incas did not understand the principle of the wheel. Roads were therefore made for pack-carrying llamas, for those foot travelers who had been given permission by the government to use the highways, and for the Inca's army.

Along the highways were *tampus* (TAM-poos), or way stations, placed conveniently a day's journey apart. Beside the *tampus* were government storehouses which could supply an army of about

*Inca road symbols: (A) a royal* tampu; *(B) a stopping place for less important people; (C) an auxiliary halting place. (According to Poma de Ayala.)*

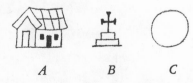

A          B          C

25,000 men. Cities along these roads contained royal *tampus* for the Inca's use when he traveled. These luxurious royal rest houses were kept always in readiness for the emperor's visit.

Work crews, recruited from the local *ayllus*, built new roads and kept existing ones in repair. These work crews were overseen by government engineers sent from Cuzco. Sometimes portions of the road were paved with stone, but stones were not available at many places along the coast.

At times the road might be only 36 inches wide and cut out of solid rock. Parts of the coastal road were as wide as 15 feet. Causeways were built over marshes, and bridges were suspended over rivers and canyons. Many of these amazing suspension bridges were kept in repair and used even during Spanish colonial times. One such 250-foot-long bridge, spanning the Apurimac River, lasted from 1350 to 1890, with its main cables being renewed every two years.

These bridges were usually built of five great cables made of braided or twisted fibers taken mostly from a plant, maguey (ma-GAY), that is still used for making rope. Cables, often as thick as a man's body, were stretched across ravines, and the ends were attached to beams that had been sunk into great piles of stones and earth. Smaller ropes or vines laced the three floor cables to the two hand cables. Mud and matting were placed over the floor cables. Although suspension bridges swayed dangerously, both men and llamas passed over them safely.

The Incas also used pontoon bridges made of reed boats strapped

*A suspension bridge in the Apurimac region.*

together and covered with mud and grasses. Another bridge, a sort of breeches buoy or basket in which the traveler sat hunched up, was used. The basket, suspended from a cable, was drawn across a ravine by a bridge attendant.

The runners called *chasquis* ran swiftly over the royal roads and bridges, taking messages and small packages from town to town, province to province, and to the Lord Inca in Cuzco. These couriers frequently carried *quipus*, the dangling, knotted strings used for counting and for keeping records.

At one- to two-and-a-half-mile intervals along the road were two little stations, facing each other on either side of the track. Within each sat two runners who watched and waited for the approach of a courier. When the panting runner appeared, one of the waiting men sprang up and ran alongside him to receive the spoken message, *quipu*, or package, and carry it on while the winded runner stopped to rest. The fresh runner was relieved in turn after his dash down the road to the next relay post. It has been said that *chasquis* could run between Lima and Cuzco, a distance of 420 miles, in three days and that the Lord Inca had fresh fish brought to him in two days from the coast — a distance of 130 miles. It would seem that these couriers were capable of running a mile in six and a half minutes. *Chasquis* served for periods of fifteen days at a time. This service was their labor tax.

Getting from place to place easily and quickly and receiving messages in a hurry were all-important to the government. If rebellion smoldered in a far-off province, the Inca quickly sent his troops. Their unexpected early arrival damped down trouble. By

*The ruins of Muyocmarca ("Circular Enclosure"). This is one of three towers on the top of the fortress Sacsahuamán. It was used as a water reservoir, and pipes led from it to other parts of the fortress.*

much the same means enemy nations were often surprised before they were ready to meet an invading Inca army.

The Incas' vast network of roads joined together hundreds of villages and cities. The cities had nearby *pucaras* (poo-KA-ras), or hilltop fortresses. The *pucaras* were often miniature cities in themselves, complete with a sun temple, houses, and reservoirs for water, as well as barracks for troops. When an enemy threatened, the city people fled to the safety of their *pucaras*.

Perhaps the most amazing piece of architecture in all the Americas is a *pucara* called Sacsahuamán. This great fort stands on the

*The ruins of the* pucara *at Ollantaytambo. Steep terraces lead up to this fortress and to the six giant stones which were to have formed the base of a sacred sun temple.*

edge of a high hill above Cuzco. Cieza de León wrote that thirty thousand Indians took seventy years to build it.

Sacsahuamán has three terraced walls facing a flat plaza. The walls are over a third of a mile long and are set in a pattern that zigzags over the ground like the teeth of a saw. Each wall is about 20 feet high. This fort has only three entrances. It has been reported that the first wall contains some blocks of stone that are 20 feet high, 14 feet wide, 12 feet deep, and some 200 tons in weight. The top terrace has a water reservoir. Pipes formerly brought water to it from higher reservoirs nearly two miles away. At one time Sacsahuamán had three fortified towers, but only traces of them remain today.

Ollantaytambo was another *pucara*, located northwest of Cuzco near the Urubamba River. This fort protected the Incas from raids by the fierce northern tribes. Here one can see six gigantic stones that were intended to be the base of a sun temple. It was never completed because the Spanish arrived first.

Farther north the Urubamba River races into a gorge. High above the river, clinging to the steep sides of the mountains that form this gorge, are a series of fortresses about ten or twelve miles apart and joined by a stone-paved road. They are Huamanmarca, Patallacta, Winay-whayna, Botamarca, and Loyamarca. These forts lead to Machu Picchu, the famous stone citadel that was never found by the Spaniards.

Machu Picchu stands hidden some two thousand feet above the Urubamba River, between two mountain peaks. It was discovered by Hiram Bingham in 1911, while he was searching for Vilcapampa, another Inca stronghold. Machu Picchu contained terraces for farming, thatched houses, barracks for soldiers, temples, sacred plazas, and royal residences. The town's water supply came by means of a stone aqueduct, from springs about a mile away. Just inside the city wall the water was channeled to fall over steps into a series of sixteen stone basins, one lower than the other. This unique water system is called the Stairway of the Fountains. Women filled their water jars at these stone basins. Today this city of stone build-

55

*Machu Picchu, with a view of the needle-like mountain Huayna Picchu in the background.*

*This doorway at Machu Picchu shows the Incas' finely fitted stonework and their characteristic opening, narrower at the top. This Machu Picchu doorway could be locked with a wooden gate held by ropes which passed through the stone ring above it and by ropes which passed through the thick stones on either side.*

ings is being restored by archeologists and Indian workers. The roofs of some buildings have even been rethatched, so that Machu Picchu looks very much as it did over four hundred years ago.

Inca towns and cities usually contained a great plaza bordered with a sun temple and palaces. Roads led away from this plaza to other streets and to the houses of the lesser nobles. On the outskirts of the town were the houses of the peasants.

The finest Inca buildings were built of carefully cut and polished stone. No cement was used to hold the stones together. It is amazing that the Incas could build as they did, since most of their tools were also made of stone.

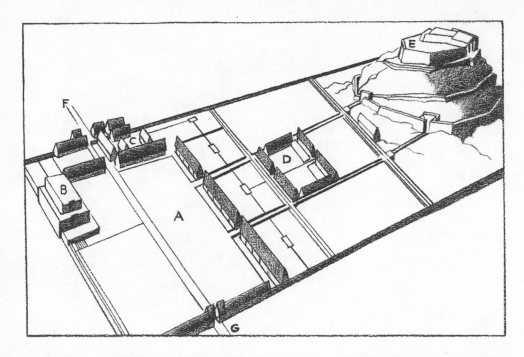

*Cajamarca, according to archeological ruins and old records, contained (A) a great plaza; (B) an interior fortress; (C) the Inca's quarters; (D) the House of the Chosen Women; (E) the fortress (pucara); (F) a road to Cuzco; (G) a road from the north.*

*The Incas' trapezoidal niche is found in nearly all their buildings.*

Building stones were quarried and then placed on rollers to which ropes were attached. Men pulled the stones to the building site. Here each stone was shaped and polished by skilled stone-cutters who chipped at the rough surface of the rock with stone tools and rubbed it smooth with abrasives such as sand. Each stone was then hoisted with ropes up an earth ramp and was fitted exactly to the stone next it on the building, probably by rubbing the two stones together. The fitting was so exact that even today a knife blade cannot be inserted between them.

New Inca cities were planned by government architects, who first worked with small clay models. The cities were built by local people, as part of their work tax, under the direction of government architects and overseers. Archeologists and explorers have studied many Inca cities, including Limatambo, Vilcashuaman, Huánaco, Cajamarca, Tumipampa, and the recently discovered Vilcapampa. Vilcapampa is thought to be the last stronghold of the defeated Incas, and a hiding place the Spaniards never found.

Many Inca buildings have all but disappeared because their stones have been removed by later peoples to make new structures, or because trees, vines, and grass have grown up through them and have toppled them over.

The architecture of the Inca Empire had a special mark: openings in the buildings were trapezoidal — narrower at the top. Sometimes the windows were blind: that is, they were not really windows with openings, but were only niches. Nearly all Inca buildings have windows, niches, or doorways that are trapezoidal.

In addition to architecture and engineering the Incas knew something about astronomy. They had a twelve-month calendar, probably with each month reckoned from new moon to new moon. The twelve-month year reckoned by the moon's phases did not entirely agree with the solar year, so it is likely that the Incas added some extra days occasionally, to make their monthly calendar agree with the seasons. It is thought that the ninth Inca, Pachacuti, had four stone towers built on the skyline east and west of the valley city of Cuzco. By observing the rising and setting sun from a point in the city's great square, in relation to these towers, astronomers could mark the changing seasons.

The artists of the Incas produced fine weaving, metalworking, and pottery. Women did nearly all the spinning and they wove cloth on looms, using the wool of the alpaca, llama, and vicuña, and also using cotton from the coast. The women used a backstrap loom. One end of the loom was tied to a tree or a post, while the other end was tied to a band around the weaver's back. By moving back from the tree the weaver was able to tighten the threads on

*An Inca backstrap loom. In addition to weaving wools and cotton, many Inca people worked with colorful jungle-bird feathers, interweaving them into the fabric.*

the loom. As her work progressed, the cloth was rolled up on the lower loom bar, and new threads were unwound from the upper loom bar. The backstrap loom could not produce pieces of cloth that measured more than 30 inches wide — about the span of the weaver's arms.

Dyes were made mostly from plants: indigo for blue, achiote for red. Along the coast certain shellfish were used for dyeing fabrics. Besides this, cotton came in a variety of natural shades ranging from white to rusty-brown to gray.

The designs of Inca weaving and pottery were mostly geometric.

*(A) This jar, called an* aryballus, *has the pointed, conelike bottom, vertical handles, and tall neck typical of this form of Inca pottery. Most Inca pottery is painted in geometric designs. (B) A stone container in the form of an alpaca.*

*The* kero *is an Inca goblet carved from wood and decorated with painted designs.*

Commonly made pieces of pottery were *aryballuses* (ar-y-BAL-lus-es), pointed-base jars, each with a knob around which a rope was probably wound for carrying purposes; and pitchers. The Incas painted their pottery with red, white, and black colors, and sometimes with yellow and orange, in small repeated designs. In addition to the pottery, flat-bottomed stone dishes, and wooden drinking cups called *keros*, were much used.

Gold was used only by the Lord Inca and the aristocracy. It was often pounded into thin sheets and used for plating the walls of palaces or temples. Masks, earplugs, goblets, plates, statues, and ceremonial knives were also made from both gold and silver. Some tools and weapons were made from copper and bronze.

According to Garcilaso de la Vega, Huayna Capac, the eleventh emperor, had a chain of gold 700 feet long. It was used in a ceremonial dance in the great square at Cuzco. Each link was as big as a man's wrist, and the chain was so heavy that two hundred Indians had difficulty in carrying it. This chain, if it ever existed, was never found by the gold-loving Spaniards.

## THE EMPIRE BUILDERS AND THE SPANISH

Before the rule of Pachacuti, the ninth Lord Inca, the Inca state was a tiny, struggling one, engaged in small wars with its neighbors. Our story begins here with Viracocha Inca, Pachacuti's father, two centuries after the founding of Cuzco by Manco Capac.

According to legend, Viracocha Inca, eighth lord, had a son he did not like. This young prince, pale and bearded, was a troublemaker, and his father exiled him to a llama ranch far from Cuzco. Three years later, Viracocha's son reappeared and told his father that he had seen a vision while sleeping in a pasture. A bearded man in robes, leading an unknown animal, appeared before him, saying he was the Creator, Viracocha, and that enemies of the Inca were raising an army to destroy Cuzco. Thinking his son was mad, the Lord Inca sent the prince back into exile. Some months later, however, three powerful tribes sent thirty thousand soldiers against the capital. Frightened, Viracocha Inca and his family fled from

63

*The Temple of the Moon at Pachacamac, near present-day Lima. Pachacamac was a famous religious shrine which attracted thousands of pilgrims.*

Cuzco, but the exiled prince returned and rallied his people to face their enemies. By the end of the day thirty thousand men lay dead on the plain, but the prince and his brave followers had won. In 1438 the prince became the ninth Inca and took the name of Pachacuti.

Under Pachacuti's rule the empire soon spread from Lake Titicaca in the southeast to Lake Junin in the northwest. In 1463, Pachacuti's son, Topa Inca, took charge of the army. Father and son worked together and the empire grew even greater.

Topa Inca fought northward almost to present-day Quito, in Ecuador, and then wheeled his army down the coast, where he persuaded the powerful Chimu people to join the empire. He then drove further south to Pachacamac, below present-day Lima. His father, Pachacuti, remained behind in Cuzco to organize the ever expanding empire and to rebuild the capital.

In about 1471, Pachacuti retired and Topa Inca became the ruler. He continued his conquests of the southern coast of Peru and the northern parts of what are now Bolivia, Argentina, and Chile.

In 1493, Huayna Capac became the eleventh Lord Inca when his father Topa Inca died. He conquered the highlands of Ecuador, beyond Quito. But Huayna Capac was more an administrator than a warlord.

Toward the end of Huayna Capac's reign a strange rumor came to the royal court. The Inca's armies had made a forced march south to quell an uprising. They arrived there to discover that the rebellious Indians were accompanied by a strange-looking man who was white and wore a beard. This Spanish adventurer had been shipwrecked on the coast of Brazil and later had been captured by the Indians. He was the first white man to be seen by the Incas.

Other reports came to Huayna Capac about pale men in "sea houses," or boats. Finally thirteen white men landed at Tumbes. This was the first Spanish expedition to the land of the Incas. Huayna Capac did nothing, and the Spanish soon left.

In 1525, Huayna Capac died during an epidemic which may have been smallpox or measles, both white men's diseases introduced by the Spanish. His death brought on a time when the empire was divided. One son, Atahualpa, ruled the north and lived in Quito. Another, Huascar, ruled the south from Cuzco. The two brothers reigned for some time, but suspicion, treachery, and ambi-

*One of the three gateways to Sacsahuamán, the gigantic fortress outside of Cuzco.*

tion filled their hearts. Atahualpa had his father's great army, which was still at Quito, following an earlier campaign. Two great generals, Quisquis and Challcuchima, were his friends. Finally war broke out and Atahualpa rallied his father's army against Huascar. This civil war lasted for several years.

Huascar's army marched north to meet that of Atahualpa at Riobamba. The fierce battle was won by Atahualpa's forces, as were several other engagements. Triumphant, Atahualpa moved his troops south to make his headquarters at Cajamarca. Huascar again set out to meet his brother's troops. The two armies met at Cotabamba, a town not far from Cuzco on the banks of the Apurimac River. Huascar won the first day's battle, but on the second day many of his soldiers were ambushed in a ravine and slaughtered.

Huascar himself was captured by Atahualpa's general, Challcuchima. On hearing that their emperor had been taken, Huascar's men fled. The victorious army camped on the outskirts of Cuzco. Atahualpa, new Lord Inca, ordered that all members of Huascar's family be executed and that Huascar be imprisoned. He was later killed by order of Atahualpa.]

News of his army's victory had come to Atahualpa in Cajamarca just at the time when he heard of a second appearance of white men on the coast. He decided not to return to Cuzco until these strange people left, as they had five years before.

In May, 1532, 180 Spanish foot soldiers and cavalrymen had landed above the coastal city of Tumbes. Their leader was the ambitious, fearless Francisco Pizarro, who sought gold and power. Pizarro knew of the war between the two brothers. With 62 horsemen, 106 infantry soldiers, and a few small cannon which shot stone balls, he marched toward Cajamarca. On November 15, 1532, this tiny army entered the deserted city. The Lord Inca and his force of 30,000 men were camped on the plains outside Cajamarca, It is believed that Atahualpa expected the Spaniards to surrender.

Pizarro sent two captains, Hernando de Soto and Hernando Pizarro, his brother, with thirty-five horsemen to Atahualpa's camp to arrange a meeting. The Incas had never before seen horses, and when de Soto galloped his horse toward Atahualpa and his courtiers, some of the men shrank back in fear. The horse was pulled up just inches from the Lord Inca, who never flinched. It is said that afterward Atahualpa beheaded those who had shown fear.

*The Spanish conquistadores were met on the beach near Tumbes by Indians, who were amazed at the white men's beards and clothing. (Redrawn from Poma de Ayala.)*

The emperor agreed to meet the Spanish commander the following day.

Throughout the night Pizarro laid his plans while his tiny band of soldiers polished their weapons. The following afternoon the Lord Inca, seated on a throne of gold borne by nobles, approached the city with five thousand men. Pizarro's men were hidden around the great square. When Atahualpa entered, this square was empty. He asked, "Where are the strangers?" and his attendants answered that the Spaniards were afraid.

Presently the Spanish priest, Valverde, approached the Inca party. With him was an Indian boy who spoke Spanish and Quechua. Valverde explained that Spain and its king were now rulers of the land. He held out a prayer book to Atahualpa, but according to some historians the Lord Inca threw it to the ground.

A shot was fired and the Spanish battle cry, "*Santiago*," filled the square. Spanish crossbows, cannons, and muskets rained death on the bewildered Indians. Atahualpa was dragged from his golden litter and made a prisoner, while his army fled in terror. Over two thousand Indians were killed.

Soon after his capture, Atahualpa realized that, most of all, the Spanish wanted gold. He decided to ransom himself by promising Pizarro enough gold and silver to fill his cell as high as his hand could reach — over seven feet. Pizarro agreed, and word went out to every corner of the empire. For two months, gold and silver poured into Cajamarca on the backs of llamas and people, until the line drawn high on the wall was reached.

*Atahualpa reaches up the wall of his prison in Cajamarca to show how much gold he will give the Spaniards if they will release him. This "ransom room" may still be seen. (Redrawn from Poma de Ayala.)*

Inca goldsmiths were kept busy for over a month melting down beautiful gold and silver works of art. The molten metal was then cast into bars. These were divided among Pizzaro's men after one-fifth of the ransom had been set aside for Charles V, King of Spain. It has been estimated that Atahualpa's ransom came to over eight million dollars.

Although the Lord Inca was declared free he remained a prisoner. The Spanish were afraid of a native uprising and soon decided that it would be wiser if he were put to death. Atahualpa was given a choice: if he accepted Christianity, the Spaniards would strangle him rather than burn him at the stake. The last Lord Inca was strangled and died in the summer of 1533.

For years after Atahualpa's death the Inca people, led by Manco Inca, a half brother of Huascar, and by his sons, tried to restore the empire, but the Spanish forces grew stronger and the Inca people gradually lost their will to fight. Finally Topa Amaru, leader of a band who still resisted the Spanish, was executed in Cuzco in 1572.

In less than one hundred years the Incas had forged a mighty empire of nearly six million people, and that same empire had been toppled almost overnight by an army of less than two hundred Spanish adventurers.

## A List of Inca Rulers

1. Manco Capac (A.D. 1250*)
2. Sinchi Roca
3. Lloque Yupanqui
4. Mayta Capac
5. Capac Yupanqui
6. Inca Roca
7. Yahuar Huacac
8. Viracocha Inca
9. Pachacuti (*1438-1471*)
10. Topa Inca (*1471-1493*)
11. Huayna Capac (*1493-1525)
12. Huascar (1525-1532)
13. Atahualpa (1525-1532)

## Chronology

1250*   The Incas enter Cuzco.
1400*   Viracocha Inca becomes the ruler.
1438*   Pachacuti becomes emperor.
1463*   Topa Inca commands the army.
1471*   Topa Inca succeeds his father to the throne.
1492    Columbus discovers America.
1493*   Topa Inca dies and is succeeded by Huayna Capac.
1511*   Huayna Capac goes north to battle the Indians of Ecuador.
1513    Balboa discovers the Pacific Ocean.
1524-25 Francisco Pizarro's first voyage.
1525*   Huayna Capac dies.
1527    Pizarro reaches the coast of Peru.
1530    War of the two brothers, Atahualpa and Huascar.
1532    Pizarro returns to conquer and loot coastal region of Peru.
1532    Atahualpa is captured.
1533    Atahualpa is killed.
* Approximate dates.

# INDEX

74

77